GET OUT THE WAY

Insights into Personal & Organizational Resistance to Change

Dr. M.R. Clarke

Printed in the United States of America

Scripture quotations marked KJV are from the King James Version of the Bible

ISBN 978-0-578-95888-0   ebook
ISBN 978-0-578-96446-1   print

I dedicate this book to my Family & Friends.

May all your dreams come to fruition,

as you balance wisdom with passion.

I LOVE YOU !

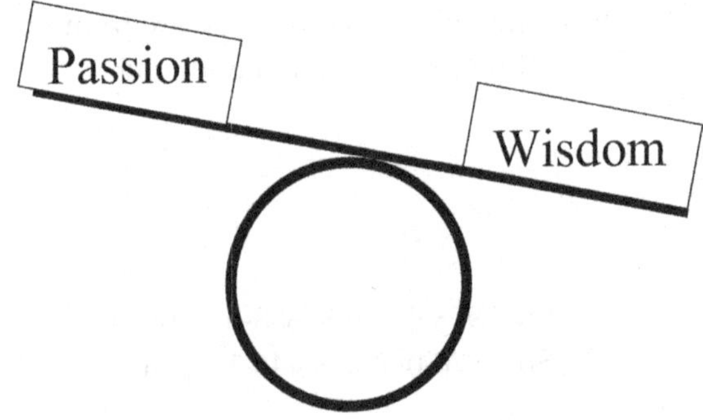

"The Events of the past do not have to
define who we are and, for that matter,
who we want to be."   DRMRCLARKE

CONTENTS

INTRODUCTION

"For Everything there is a season" Ecclesiastes 3:1-8

Our grandparent's generation dreamed of a better life for their kids. Our grandparent's kids who would become our parent's generation also wanted a better life for us. However, there is no way to see the dreams of our grandparents and our parents come to pass without change. One might argue that change is neither good or bad and the definition would be limited to how each person perceives said change. I studied accounting at Morehouse College, and I might add, my days at Da House looked nothing like the Morehouse College of today. That is hopefully, change to be expected. One generation leaving a legacy for the next to improve upon. One of the terms learned during a study of international business was Kaizen. We learned Kaizen is the Japanese term used in business to describe the pursuit and attainment of operational excellence. Kaizen means "change for the better" or "continuous improvement." At the core of Kaizen is the principle that every component of the production process has a voice. Every employee that touches the production of the product can, at any moment, stop the process to call out issues no matter how small. The idea is that everyone has a vested interest is producing the best product or service possible. This not only creates a quality product or service, but it also develops great pride in being a part of the production team. Corporations bought into the Kaizen concept in the 1980s. Non-profits and Non-Governmental organizations could learn a lot from implementing the Kaizen Principle. That is, if we were not so resistant to change.

This book is written to speak to both personal and organizational resistance to growth. At the core of growth is the proverbial process of change. Change, in and of itself, is neither good or bad. One's perception of change is influenced by many factors. I write *GET OUT THE WAY*, in part, due to the frustrations of dealing with non-profit organizations made up of volunteers who get involved and participate for a variety of reasons and, oftentimes, hidden agendas. As well, Get Out The Way is written due to my own occasional disillusionment from purpose, stemming from working with a variety of leadership styles in organizations and corporations that have narrow, outdated systems, and incompetent levels of abilities, if any. There seems to be ample opportunity to revamp methods and operations, however no one takes the steps or initiatives to change. Also, in my personal life, I can identify periods where I was stuck on stupid making unwise and foolish decisions. I will talk more about why I use the word decisions instead of choices in chapter three. When I look back on my life, I ask the question, what was I ever thinking? Why did I hang out with her or why did I do that with him? Why did I not make the change back then? There has got to be a better way people! No doubt you and others can relate.

There are so many reasons why change in life is so very unwelcomed. GET OUT THE WAY looks at the journey of change from a personal and experiential perspective. The goal of Get Out The Way is to offer insights regarding why individuals and institutions have such unnaturally high levels of resistance to change and how we all might embrace the process of change in order to grow and be successful.

Chapter one is entitled Change in the Background. A summary history of change is discussed. Chapter two is entitled Identifying why humans do not like change. Human beings are creatures of habit and there are a lot of fears people have that keeps change from occurring. Some are real and far too many are not so real. Too often, many choose to stay in the ignorant category which is, not knowing the difference between real fear and false evidence appearing real. This keeps us from getting involved in really living. The problem with staying ignorant is that choosing to deny change happens or has happened, argues against the fact that change occurs in everything and everyone, including ourselves.

Chapter three is entitled Coping with Change. You cannot change the seasons of life, but you can change you. Chapter four is entitled Going FWD. The Peter principle is a concept in management developed by Laurence J. Peter, which observes that people in a hierarchy tend to rise to their "level of incompetence". In other words, an employee is promoted based on their success in previous jobs until they reach a level at which they are no longer competent, as skills in one job does not necessarily translate to another.

Once you have received the insights to why we resist change outlined is this book, you are ready to Get Out the Way. (1) Ready to Get Out the Way of God; (2) Ready to Get Out the

Way of yourself; (3) Ready to Get Out the Way, especially, of those coming up behind you; Going Fwd challenges you to grow forward into the future by embracing the process of change. All scripture references are from the King James version of the Bible found in the public domain. Now let me Get Out the Way as you dive into the pages of this book shared from the heart and the many vicissitudes in life.

Chapter 1:

CHANGE IN THE BACKGROUND

"Remember it is the LORD God who gives you the power to get wealth"

Deuteronomy 1:18(KJV)

Clay Evans sang a Gospel song in 1995 that illustrates the power that comes from reflecting on all of life's changes. The lyrics are: "As I look back over my life, And I think things over. I can truly say that I've been blessed, I've got a testimony." The powerful message of this song speaks to looking back at one's life and appreciating the journey. Too many people look back on their life but only see the pain, heart ache and loss. Appreciation of the journey is often only found in a minority of the population. Life's reflection is often focused on the negative. Too often we dwell on experiences that remind us of what we lost and what we do not have. Thankfully, I've got a testimony expresses that I have gone through some stuff in life, and I am yet alive to talk about it.

For many, testimony is used in place of the word 'story.' What is the difference you may be asking? Well, a testimony is to inspire or encourage others by seeing the power of a universal Force that is recognized and at work in one's experience. In other words, the universal Force is present in my life and is present in your life such that you can be encouraged to not give up and to endure until change comes.

During my freshman year at Morehouse College, the professor gave an assignment to research the events in history for the year of our birth. My initial thought was that does not sound very interesting, but in the process of researching 1965, I found that, at the time of my birth, so many historic events were happing. The main take away of the assignment was that 1965 was a time of great change. I do not know where that hard copy of the assignment is, but history is still frozen in the past for any seeker to find. Technology today gives the seeker access to information at the speed of light with one touch of their fingertips. However, the countless hours viewing microfiche, searching out books in the library developed the seeker in me that does not settle for the quick answers in life. Here are some of the interesting events of change for 1965 my research found outlined in onthisday.com:

- *President Johnson's "Great Society" State of Union Address*
- *Supremes release "stop in the Name of Love"*
- *Malcolm X is shot dead*
- *1st person to walk in space was from Soviet Union*
- *1st US Senate black page, Lawrence W Bradford, Jr at age 16*
- *Mariner IV sends back 1st pictures of Mars*
- *Mobutu Sese Seko Kuku Ngbendu becomes President of Zaire*

Looking back to see the history of our birth year is very cool. The above seven events of 1965 demonstrates that America and the World was experiencing lots of change. I wonder if the grown-ups of 1965 were looking ahead fifty years to all the new advancements in the world their innovation and creativity produced? I am sure not many were looking towards the future in that way.

The concept of change is none debatable as the evidence of change occurring is all around us. For example: I remember watching a movie where a little boy remembered how his father would mark the boy's height each year on his birthday. Years later when the boy grew up, [note the direction up] he returned to the house and found the height markings still there showing how much taller he grew from year to year. I took my que from that movie and measured and marked my height on the door post of my room. I check from day to day and saw no change. I did not understand then why my mom did not like the pen markings on the door post of my room in the apartment we were renting. I now understand, we did not own it and she would have to pay to paint/repair when we moved. If you missed it, in the movie the boy's height was marked in the home he grew up in to indicate his height change from year to year. Although I made the marks on the door post, I was unable to see any change because I did not give the change process time to occur.

As a side note, when renting a home or apartment, one should not put marks or damage the property as there is a cost to repair and replace when you move out or 'change' where you live. For that matter, do not even mark up the walls and door post if you purchase the property. Why? Start looking at all real estate as an investment. That is, at some point in the future, the buildup of equity or value of the property can be accessed from loans using the property as collateral.

Or you can pull out the equity by selling the property. Equity is the difference between what you paid for the property and its increased value in the open market. This kind of preparing for change we will discuss later in chapter four. If you say what is the point in owning a home if I cannot make it my own, then I would say to you, go right ahead. Mark up and do whatever you feel will make it yours. Just be prepared to shell out the cash in repairs because a buyer probably would not want to buy what is your kind of home. Granted, everyone will not purchase a home with the intent of selling it to realize a cash profit that is tax exempt. During the writing of this book in 2019, I believe any profits made from the sale of your primary home that is less than $250,000 is considered tax free. Check with your tax preparer to give you the appropriate tax rule. In any event, remember that owning land and or real estate is the quickest path to wealth. Get Out the Way of change and be wealthy.

The previous paragraph has multiple examples of change. Did you notice them? 'I remembered' indicating a different mental location in the past; the boy remembered his father; the father marked the height to show height changes; the boy returned after some years, and so on. The main point is that change is so constant and is such a normal part of our lives that we overlook the evidence of change and what I call 'true reality.' Whenever you overlook a 'thing' (a principle), it is our choices that kicks against immoveable truths. Fear of change is therefore not of every form of change but rather it is fear of big and drastic change that pulls or pushes us from our comfortable perceptions of life. We do not fear changing our clothes or the ink in the printer. To that point, we may fear not having any clean clothes to change into or may fear the ink running out in the printer before we print out an important document we are working on.

By now each of you should pick up on the word 'remember.' Remember is the act of looking back on one's life and experiences. For most people, images and movie like pictures appear in our mind's eye. We see our past and, often-times, feel as though we are back in a specific moment. When I look at myself, I imagine there is a huge painting of my life in the background. When we remember, we take our focus off the present moment and step back into the past. The problem with memory is that there is change in the past. That is, our memory of the past also changes as time goes on. You may have heard the principle that says, "we do not remember what was said or what was done to us; we remember how someone made us feel." So then, since memory is tied to feeling, then what I remember will depend on how I felt about the experience. Another way of making this point is the way I think or interpret the past event or experience has everything to do with how I choose to remember. How I choose to remember is connected to my interpretation or thoughts about the event. The event could have been years ago and yet I may still have strong feelings about it.

A great example of how our experience is linked to our emotions is that of two college friends who have not spoken in 15 years. They meet each other at the college homecoming football game. After the game they go out to eat and decide to clear up any bad blood they have between them. One starts by sharing what they remember the reason for not talking for 15 years. The other is shocked as they remember the reason being something totally different. Who is right and who is wrong? Well, they both are. Since both were hurt emotionally, they carried the separate and different feelings of what happened and the memories they thought were accurate. Whatever the actual event, time changed their memories just enough that locked their feelings of hurt in their minds and was manifested in the form of not communicating with each other

for 15 years. Realizing neither could remember

why they were angry with the other, both

estranged friends laughed and felt bad that

they wasted all those years being angry with

each other.

Thinking about the past is all about reflecting on what has already happened. Reflection or remembrance occurs so that we can be the best of who we are in the

"the events of the past do not have to define who we are and for that matter who we want to be."
Dr. MRClarke

present. If we do not look far enough back in our past, who we become is significantly limited when we do not work with the full picture of what has happened. A black man who had multiple advanced degrees and was working for a big corporation once said to me that he was from South Carolina, not Africa. After speaking with him at length, I realized that his interpretation of his past began and ended with where he and his parents were born. Not embracing the past beyond his place of birth did not stop his personal success, however, the way he felt about who he is, limited the degree of success he could experience on a cultural and community basis.

Many studies have confirmed that we hire people who look like we do. A Forbes article published online on May 1, 2008, by Kimberly Giles concluded, "unconscious bias toward people who are of the same race, education level, economic status and have the same personality, fears or values influences who you hire much more than you think." Not embracing history beyond the place of birth does not make a person bad. However, not embracing one's full and complete ancestry, severely limits the access to the power of who one truly is.

The final part of why we do not like change has to do with ignorance. Remember, ignorance is not knowing. This reminds me of the popular saying, "we do better, when we know better." So then, we do not like change because we do not know that we do not know. History records that after WWII ended, fighting on some islands in the Pacific continued. Why? Because some Japanese soldiers were dug into their caves and were so disconnected from the flow of communication, that they continued to fight, holding on to the last word or command that was given to them.

We do the same in our personal and organizational affairs. We dig down deep into our emotional dysfunction and keep fighting from the last point of pain in the past or the last betrayal of a boss or family member. We become so imbedded in our hate, anger, and depression that the negative emotions become our normal way of feeling and living. There is no way we can ready ourselves to embrace change when we feel more alive drowning in emotional pain that is pinned up inside. We hold on tight to past emotional thoughts and experiences which fuels our rage to resist any change. This eats us up from inside out. I declare, now is the moment to Get Out the Way of past relationship pain and let go of the stories we tell ourselves of the past that keep

us stuck in toxic feelings. Once I let go of the

need to re-live toxic feelings day in and day

out, I only then will start to live my best life.

Change in the past is about recognizing

that the events of the past do not have to define

who we are and for that matter who we want

to be. The Power to Be our true selves is

found, in part and parcel from recognizing that

we each have the ability and power in us to

create our own lives. This quote by Abraham

Lincoln captures the life application of

recognizing what happened is in the past: "The

best way to predict your future is to create it."

There is no way you can create your future by

clinging on to all the stuff that has happened in

your past. Well, yes you can create a future by clinging to past hurt, but that future will simply continue to look like everything in your past. The failures, the doubts, the heartbreaks, the toxic relationships, and the self-sabotage will continually occur and define your feelings and perceptions of life. Our internal dialogue or voices in our head wants us to do everything 'other' than Get Out the Way of toxic feelings created from past experiences. Understanding better how our resistance to let go of past hurt impacts our ability to walk powerfully in the present, improves a person's response to when change happens.

Chapter 2:

PEOPLE DO NOT LIKE CHANGE

"Behold I DO A New Thing" Isaiah 43:19

The first step in getting out of the way is to understand why we do not like change. Change is so uncomfortable, isn't it? Truth be told, change is most uncomfortable when you fight against it. When you take the perspective that 'I will embrace change,' the actual change process often-times becomes a wonderful experience. So, behold I do a new thing in Isaiah 43:19 could perhaps be a revealing declaration from God outlining that

> "The new thing (principle) the Creator wants us to see is, the unseen power in us is greater than anything we see outside of ourselves."
> DR.MRClarke

we are encouraged to embrace the new thing
or principle. What is the new thing? The new
thing or principle the Creator wants us to see
is, "the unseen power in each of us is greater
than anything we see outside of ourselves."
Dr. Joe Dispenza is an author who teaches that
our daily thinking are simply thoughts which
are mostly of the past. These thoughts produce
feelings that direct our actions. Dr. Dispenza
says that we can create good healthy attitudes
by understanding that human beings have a
distinction from other species because we can
change our thinking which changes our
feelings and how we see ourselves and the
world we live in. Some scientists say all
species on Earth have evolved from something

or another.   Science has shown how a cat from today evolved from a prehistoric cat; the crocodile is said to be closely related to some pre-historic dinosaur. The Webster Dictionary defines evolution as "the gradual development of something, especially from a simple to a more complex form. This book does not get tangled up in the debate of whether humans evolved from a cell or not. Let it be sufficient to ask however, who created the first spark to get a big bang process started? The cell did not say to itself, 'I will be.' Looking at the splendor of Nature sure makes believing in a Great Creator so much easier. So then, here is something to think about. Is God's new thing calling on us to see that we are different from other species because we have the God Source in us, giving us the ability to not be defined by what is happening around us? If you accept this as truth, then why do we not like change? I submit to you that we do not like change because of our 'ignorance.' We simply do not know how powerful we are. Oh yes, I must invoke the famous quote from Marianne Williamson.

"Our deepest fear is not that we are inadequate. Our deepest fear is that we are powerful beyond measure. It is our light, not our darkness, that most frightens us."

We fear change because we do not like when we do not know; we do not trust what we cannot see. We tell ourselves that life is better if we do not make the change.   I know, those of the Christian Belief will say, we walk by faith and not sight. Well, I get that. However, there is a pre-process everyone goes through to get to that stage of walking by faith. The process involves understanding the internal thoughts we have regarding the unknown and coping with the uncertainty of the future. All the emotions that have to do with change come into play whether we are aware of them or not. A Christian who feels anxious or scared about taking a step is still a Christian. In fact, the Creator knowing this has said 365 times in scripture, "do not be afraid." To my count, that means one reminder per day to us all, do not be afraid. The Creator reminding us of this reality means Believers do get anxious and are sometimes scared. So then, it is so much wiser to accept that the process of walking by Faith will include life application skills of how to cope with change.

We do not like change because we hold onto the status quo and the way things are. Never mind things were not always like this. A review of an English translation dictionary reveals that the Latin meaning of status quo is "the mess we're in." It seems that we get so used to the way things are that we become resistant to change. So, we hold on and stay in the mess we are in, even if the mess makes us miserable. Somewhere along the way someone has told us a big fat lie that we must endure abuse because that is what people 'like us' do. People like us could mean Christians, Blacks, Mexicans, Asians, Africans, immigrants, and any stereotype you want to apply. Seems to me that the main people that do not like or want change from the status quo, are the ones in charge. That must mean that those who do not like change because they are stuck in the status quo probably think they have not only arrived but that those in charge have accepted them into their ranks. Those that have ears to hear, hope you are listening.

Ignorance is therefore bliss as the old saying goes. Pastor AR Bernard once taught that "you will not mature unless you are willing to change; that's why a stubborn person will always be an ignorant person, because they refuse to be taught." Oh yes, I certainly agree with Dr. Bernard. Let the sting of offense sit with you a moment if you have not been willing to change in some area of life. Hear me now when I say you are well on your way to fleeing ignorance by virtue of you seeking understanding and reading <u>Get Out the Way</u>. Thank you for embracing this moment's opportunity to grow and mature. Please understand that ignorance simply means 'without knowledge.' Remaining ignorant is a choice many use to avoid being held responsible for their actions in life. Ignorance is bliss because some may think that if they know to do right and still play dumb, they will not be judged in the public space. The trouble with playing ignorant is that you will still be judged by others. The weight of being held accountable to virtue and character with oneself and others can produce a powerfully resistance to change that keeps many from walking in confidence and strength.   Ignorance is bliss because no one will have high expectations of us. If my parents do not have high expectations of me, then I do not feel sad or mad when I don't do what I am supposed to do. As a matter of fact, I will not make my bed or clean my room; or wash my body because living in the lower regions of life's existence is comfortable and have become very normal to me. There is an old principle that says, "you get what you expect." Life application: children will rise to the level of behavior that is expected of them. The problem the little girl or little boy that grew up with low expectations on their lives will be the woman or man living with low expectations of themselves. And so, I still do not make my bed or clean my home or car; or wash my body much less my face,

> "you will not mature unless you are willing to change; that is why a stubborn person is will always be an ignorant person, because they refuse to be taught."
>
> AR Bernard

because I refuse to learn from my life experiences and apply the self-realization understanding that states, 'I possess the power and control over what my life looks like.' Get Out the Way of not embracing change in your life that will bring knowledge to your mind and intentional action to your life. Yes, greater expectations will be expected from you by others, but more importantly, you will have greater expectations of growth and change for yourself.

Chapter 3:

Coping with Change

"We have this treasure in earthen vessels, that the excellency of the power

may be of God, and not of us." 2 Corinthians 4:7

I have travelled the world and I am still surprised, when I return to certain country towns and parts of the city, to see that nothing has changed. I recall a USMC Colonel giving a pep talk to his Command after I gave the prayer as their Chaplain. He said, in not these exact words, You men and women have been changed by the choice you made to wear the uniform of a U.S. Marine. Some may be deciding on whether to re-enlist. "I recommend you re-enlist, not because of the any bonus monies but because, if you chose to go back home, that same bum is going to be on the same corner talking the same junk." I do not remember how many re-enlisted, but I do remember how skillfully the Colonel formed a connection with young Marines who had embraced change and transformation in their lives. The Colonel made a clear distinction between the Marines and those old friends back home who's lives showed no change.

At the core of coping with change is understanding that we cannot change situations in life, but we can change ourselves.

Dr. Morgan, who was my Doctor of Ministry Cohort leader, taught that "transition is about how you handle the change; transition starts with an ending; transition is psychological." Transition is psychological means that a person has the ability to let go of an old reality. For me, to let go of an old reality means that the promise or reward of my present reality is much more appealing than all the discomfort my choosing to change may cause. To live in the present, one must understand that we each have the power in us to choose and create our own reality.

As a Navy Chaplain, everything the Sailor or Marine shares with you is 'IRON CLAD' Confidential. This level of confidentiality allows for real honest access, as you may imagine, to the sailor or marine's heart and the sharing of their deep feelings and secrets. Most of the time, a Marine only needed to vent. In other words, they needed

someone to talk to that would not judge them

or report to their Command what might be

going on in their lives and heads. There was a

Marine who wanted to marry his new

girlfriend before he goes off to deployment.

He seeks the advice of his Chaplain who

questions whether the Marine has known his

girlfriend long enough. As pointed out by Dr.

Nate Regier in Conflict without Casualties, folk

"will always defend their choices even if they

are unwise." This Marine justified his

intensions of the heart by closing the

conversation with, "plus the (BAH) basic

assistance for housing will be able to take care

of her while I'm gone." Before you judge this

young Marine, you must know that a large percentage of our military personnel lives below the poverty line. The Basic Assistance for Housing allotment is one strategy I suspect a lot of couples have used to justify getting married. Sounds very sweet and romantic, yes? Oh, if life and marriage were so simple. LOL! Although many young Marine couples survived separation due to work ups in preparation for deployment, there are many who's marriage was incentivized by the basic housing allowance. Mostly though, the breakup of military marriages stem from the lack of preparation for changes to their lives on a weekly/monthly basis, the likes of which the civilian population could never relate to. Some

might call learning to prepare

for change is a type of pre-marital counseling.

Whatever name the preparation is given, not

going through the "men marry hoping the woman won't change; women marry hoping the man will change." Albert Einstein

process makes the

couple more

vulnerable to a

relationship break

down. Without the awareness that change will

be part of their relationship, the couple will be

more resistant to change. Because of the

discomfort that comes with change, the couple

will become blind to the principle from Albert

Einstein that states, "men marry hoping the

woman won't change and women marry hoping the woman can change the man."

The first point in understanding why people do not like change is to look at the way each person perceives change. The way you look at situations in life reveals the way you approach the concept and process of change. One certainty in life is that change will come. However, if you expect and embrace change, those internal thoughts that want you to stay in your comfort zone will not have as much influence over your perceptions and emotions. Think of it this way, if you plan for change to occur, you will be more likely to manage the change that happens. What does this look like? Embracing change is a choice, therefore, my mind and body does not experience shock when change occurs. Stressors may be present but seeing change as part of the process activates our learned coping skills that will help us in both the short and long term.

A little clarification is needed. Just thinking about something will not bring the goal to pass. For example, *just thinking about having more money will not get me more money. Just thinking about the things in my life I don't like won't change the things in my life I don't like. Only thinking I need a job will not magically get me a job.* Somewhere along our socialization process, we were told we only need to name and claim a thing, to possess a thing. There is a lot more that comes after thinking about what you want that sadly is not shared or taught.

What comes after thinking that brings about

change? Lots of Action! It is the

"regardless of your spiritual persuasion, Faith is the corresponding Action to what you Believe."
   DR.MR.CLARKE

corresponding action to what you believe in your heart that brings about a change to your situation. I saw a social

media post that was a photo of a woman

kneeling in prayer over a tiny plant. Beside

this woman was another standing over a fully

grown tomato plant with gardening tools in

her hand. The caption read, "The difference

between prayer with no Faith and Prayer with

Faith." I have taught for many years that

regardless of your spiritual persuasion, Faith is

the corresponding Action to what you Believe.
Just thinking or imagining a thing to be is only
a portion of the formula that will bring about
lasting change in your life. The reality is, we
must apply action to achieve our goals. When
no action has been attached to an expressed
desire, the change process is suffocated and
becomes contaminated with fear and self-
doubt.

Many people work hard to get more
money to pay their rent, bills, and take care of
family. Stories of hard-working people
demonstrating high levels of responsibility and
strong work ethic is always inspiring to learn
about. However, if having more money
reveals the true character of a person, then an

abundance of 'inaction' when it comes to pursuing goals, also reveals a lack of comprehension on the part of the individual regarding what really brings about the changes in life we desire. This point is real, irrespective of your ethnic affiliation. So then, create a business instead of waiting on someone to give you a job. Apply action to your dreams and be a part of bringing your dreams to pass.

You may have heard of the difference between an eagle and a vulture. An eagle seeks out the prey that is alive. A vulture looks for dead prey. I heard an unlikely successful businessman named Ubong T. King (r.i.p.) share that, "vultures wait for the left-over things of life to be given to them."

Metaphorically speaking, either you are an eagle or a vulture. You will walk in the power of the day's possibilities seeking out opportunities, or you will sit back and wait for the government or some person to give you their handouts and leftovers. Ubong concluded, "you have a vulture mindset if you are waiting for the government or your family and friends to feed you what you want."

> "We can't get rid of daily stressors completely, but endowing people with the skills to weather stressors when they happen could pay dividends in cognitive health." . Robert Stawski

So then, what is meant by, we must expect change? Expect change refers to the continual growth of self. We must expect that we were built for change and that we must embrace change. God created us to be able to cope with events in our lives. That is, our ability to respond to situations in life is part of our wiring. Coping with change is all about training oneself (spirit-mind-body) to see the power of God residing in each of us. The power in each of us is powerless when we do not know how to access and activate God's power. Once we see ourselves as powerful, we will live and experience life more powerfully.

An article by Ana Sandoiu in MedicalNewsToday.com reported on a research study about stress and concluded, "How you react to stress may predict brain health." The research led by Robert Stawski at

Oregon's State University suggests that "it is not so much the stressful events in themselves, but our reactions to them that harm our brain health." This conversation regarding coping with stress takes on a much larger importance in transforming our personal and organizational lives to GET OUT THE WAY. Expecting change then, can now be understood as embracing the need to transform our lives by the renewing of our mind. Renewing of our mind is to continually get more knowledge and deepen our understanding. The deepened understanding is not from the quantity of issues in our lives, but rather of the built-in ability to respond to whatever life brings. The more each of us understands this principle, the more we will walk and operate in heightened

abilities to manage change.

Dr. J.W. Walker once taught that "any

change has in it, grief." For example. The

body does not know the difference between the

emotional hurt of a relationship ending and the

emotional strain of closing the door on your

finger. They are both painful! So too are the

'affects' of being ignorant as it relates to the

impact of change on the mind and the body.

When change occurs, the body will tell the

mind that there will be pain. Consider the

following circumstances and how your body

will often say 'let us just stay the way we are.'

You know that smoking deteriorates our lung's

ability to breathe but the body feels good

during the inhale and will ask for another puff.
Or someone has high blood pressure but still
eats all things greasy and/or fried pork, junk
food and lots of high sugar drinks that gives
their body a sugar rush. How about this
example? He calls me ugly and stupid, but I
am afraid to be alone. Do not worry, you are
not alone in feeling any of the above. As you
can see, all the reasons and justifications you
can think of, the body will use to 'feel' a certain
way and keep you from embracing change.
Fear based thoughts are sent to the mind by
our body to reaffirm our perceptions. A
conspiracy of mind and body is then formed to
resist the process of change called our internal
dialogue. Fear of change is established as a

mind set or the way we think. Our thoughts ultimately will dismiss any steps towards embracing change, no matter how good and better for the person said change would be. Yes, you read right. The body tells your mind that the change does not feel good. Dr. Joe Dispensa explains that we allow our feelings, which he calls the body, to develop so much control over what we do and how we act. So much so that the dynamic between the body and the mind is such that our emotions become the default dictator of our behavior over and above our thinking.

Three ways to get out the way of not wanting change is to: (1) Understanding the science to change. Studies have shown that it takes an average of thirty days to change or form a habit. Most would agree that a new habit can be broken in less than thirty days by giving into our internal dialogue that tells us to return to the old norms that we are comfortable with. I recently saw an old sitcom whose plot had the character Doug experience some embarrassment from how much weight he had put on. He got so motivated to lose the weight that he went into the closet and pulled out an exercise machine. As Doug set up the machine, he suddenly stopped and felt his forehead. Right there and then, Doug left the exercise machine in the middle of the bedroom floor and climbed into bed thinking he was too ill to exercise. I laugh even now remembering the episode. Our Emotions may have held the power for the longest, but now it is time to take back control. So then, if you do not like your current situation, then change it. This point is important because of the ancient proverb that says, "a person can endure anything on Earth as long as they know how long it's going to last."

The second way of getting out the way of not wanting change is: (2) Seeing 'FEAR' for what it is. There is an acronym in society that defines FEAR as "False Evidence Appearing Real." Many have been encouraged by the words "things are not as bad as it seems." These words imply that the Sun will always come up tomorrow. Someone once said, "it's always darkest just before the dawn." So then, do not listen to the fake internal dialogue who's only agenda is to not feel any pain or discomfort that may or may not come with change.

The third way of getting out the way of not wanting change is: (3) Realizing that "Ignorance is no excuse of the law." This view that is found in the U.S. Justice System is well known and felt, one way or another, by black and brown citizens. The implication is that the Law is based on non-complexed, simple to understand, shared common values and beliefs the Law uses to justify policies of enforcement. Also implied is that the Law will be applied 'fairly' to all. The problem with this view is that the U.S. Justice System is not designed to recognize the views and values of those in the socio-economic minority category. Between the money-making process of needing a bond to get out of jail and the prison for profits business modules, the pursuit of justice looks more like preying on the poor. More on the inequities of the U.S. System in my next book coming soon. Now let us get back to the third way of getting out the way of not wanting change.

When a law is signed, it is supposed to be applied to everyone that is within the territory of the U.S. Government. The understanding is the same when it comes to 'Universal Principles' of Life. That is, you can do yourself a lot of good by getting out the way of obstacles like ignorance that keeps you from making the change with the man/woman in the mirror. What things might you be ignorant of? Glad you asked. I was having a conversation with one of my sons about making wise choices. In response to the question, why do we make poor and bad choices, my son responded, "we don't

know what we don't know." That is very deep I said. Then I said, "you are my son." I said this to him to communicate how intelligent I felt he is and to express how proud I am to be his father. It is only human to be ignorant of many things. It is foolish to be ignorant and pretend not to be. If you are ignorant of finances, relationships, or God, don't stay ignorant. The longer you remain ignorant of a matter, the more fearful you will continue to be of change. Understanding yourself and why you do what you do is key to not being ignorant. When you are informed of who you are, not who others say you are, embracing change in life becomes less challenging. Recognizing that life is a matter of choices, will set you up to better be able to deal with change in your life. Increasing your personal understanding of how you respond to change in your life, has everything to do with whether you will make progress from the change.

Progress you see, produces "happiness" in your emotional state of mind, as I once heard Tony Robbins teach. If you want to be happy, embrace change by getting out the way of mind sets and obstacles that keep you from embracing the change process in your life. There is no doubt that change is part of the process. However, transformation is the end goal.

Chapter 4:

Going Forward

Take careful exploration of who you are

and what you have been given to do." Galatians 6:4

"Gospel profited them Not, as it was not mixed with Faith..." Hebrews 4:2

Abraham Lincoln's quote of "the best way to predict the future is to create it" is jammed packed with presumptions. The statement presumes you have gone through the process of reflection and identifying

> "The best way to predict the future is to create it"
> Abraham Lincoln

unsubstantiated fears about change. The statement also presumes you have come to terms with the need to embrace change in your life or your organization as well as understanding why taking steps towards change were not taken before now. Ultimately, once you have gone through the process of change outlined is this book, you are ready to GET OUT THE WAY. Ready to Get Out the Way of God; Ready to Get Out the Way of yourself; and especially Ready to Get Out the Way of those coming up behind you.   I use the familiar count of 1,2,3 to challenge you to Get Out the Way and take great strides of faith into your future.

Going Forward with successful progress is very unlikely when you do not know who you are. The journey of getting out the way centers on the realization of one's personal or organizational identity. The problem with personal and organizational identity is that we oftentimes look outward from ourselves to determine who we are. Also, change going forward is very challenging since we tend to be comfortable in doing what we have always done. I recall a paper I wrote in college and the study I cited which concluded that men draw their identity from the jobs they do. Ask a man to introduce himself. You will most times hear, 'hello, my name is Sam, and I am a teacher." Or I am a lawyer. No Sam, your job is not who you are, it is simply what you do. Your identity has to do with the character and values you believe in. A friend of mine put it this way, "character is about the morale fiber you have." If Sam really wants to share who he is, then Sam needs to say, 'I am trustworthy' or 'I am calm.' These declarations not only reveal who he is but also how he chooses to respond to change in life. The process of going forward must include heartfelt reflection on who I am and where I am from. In this context, 'where I am from' means what are the experiences I have had in life. It does not mean where I have lodged my living. Where I am from not only speaks to what experiences I have had, but how do I interpret does experiences. Does experience shape who I am, as most cultures believe, or do I have the power to choose and define who I am?

Bishop Bronner of Word of Faith Church in Atlanta, Georgia once taught, "the benefit of reflection is evaluation and reflection turns experience into insight." That is so good! Remembering the event or experience is one thing but insight taken from the experience is what learning the lessons of life is all about. Another way of putting it is "if I knew then what I know now." Bronner went on to teach that we should be persistent to get what we want and consistent in keeping what we got. He said, "Consistency develops trustworthiness." Trust, to me, is at the root or core of any relationship. Be it personal or business related. My life application of what Bishop Bronner taught, is that a trustworthy person will be judged to be trustworthy when he/she demonstrates trustworthiness consistently in their actions. An untrustworthy person will be consistent to the extent that they will not keep their word or do their job with loyalty, professionalism, and excellence.

What does trust have to do with the process of change in personal and organizational growth? Well, without the skill set or understanding the process of change and its impact on relationships and organizational

Decisions are driven by situations and circumstances in your life.
DR. MRClarke

dynamics, our emotions would control and dictate what our reactions would be in any situation involving change. Get Out the Way is a reminder of what to do when the habitual, fear based, ignorant voices try to influence the decisions and choices you make in life. Note the distinction between the word decisions and choices. Decisions are driven by situations and circumstances in your life. A more accurate way of defining a decision is that the circumstance being faced will 'control' our emotions and the internal dialogue we give ear to. You may know the voices as, the creature of habit mindset; the fearful perceptions; the lack of insight regarding what is really happening. When you live life with your emotions running the show, the process of change and the way fwd becomes a painfully ineffective one filled with unnecessary failure and lack.

A Choice, on the other hand is not controlled by the emotions and the body. Rather, a choice is made from a sense or mindset that I have in me the power to create the life I want. I will not blame others for my choices. Instead, I will own the results and/or consequences. I will not make excuses for the position I find my life in. Instead, I will reflect and learn to increase my understanding from what I have experienced and choose to progress forward, stepping out into the power of the possibility that can only be found in this present moment. So, the difference between decision and choice is that decision relies on forces outside of self to decide the path forward and sees the experience as something happing to me. Choice is the power/force

inside of self that chooses a path forward while

declaring how I see myself such as, 'I am

strong and powerful no matter what happens.'

The choice mindset produces resiliency in me.

A group of friends got together to

brainstorm ideas of creating streams of income.

Even after taking lots of

time to arrive at the one

idea everyone could

agree on, each person

had a different

perspective on the way forward. The same

example can be applied to an organization's

executive committee trying to come up with

ideas to grow its membership. Everyone will

have their own take on the way forward.
Those that make decisions will probably have a
strong desire to keep up with the Joneses. The
organization's committee will no doubt survey
what the group across town is doing, using the
rationale that deciding on a similar plan would
produce similar results. The group of friends
that sees themselves as powerful beings will
probably choose an idea that is the riskiest but
produces the greatest return because they
believe their strength is demonstrated in their
togetherness. Similarly, the organization's
committee that understands why they are, will
choose plans and strategies that fulfill the
mission or purpose of the organization

believing that their membership growth is due to the organization fulfilling its purpose.

As a side note, the first time I ever heard the term brainstorming was when I worked as a sales representative for Maxwell House Coffee in Tampa, Florida. Looking back, I most appreciate the sales training they provided. Too bad the age of all

"A person who has a why will always be able to endure the how"
Niche

expensed paid annual sales meetings in Canada and Boca Raton are over with. As with everything, change is always present. How we handle change has everything to do with whether, or not, we reach the stage in our lives to Get Out the Way of resisting the change process. Going Forward involves the use of the lessons learned from embracing change and applying the steps of preparation that are in place to empower us to Get Out the Way.

GET OUT THE WAY OF GOD

On page 116 of his book, <u>Conflict without Casualties</u>, Dr. Nate Regier points out that "avoiding the choice to take action, let go, and move on costs companies billions of dollars a year in the form of lost opportunities, and resources wasted in predictive analyses by bringing in more consultants whose recommendations are never implemented." This is the reality I have witnessed in organizational operations and relationships I have experienced. I have had the privilege to see a multiplicity of relational conflicts in people's lives, as well as organizations over the years that usually stem from the inability to let go and move forward. As a US Navy Chaplain and life coach, I witnessed the day-to-day challenges leadership faced with diverse emotional levels of maturity in the personnel. Many resisting the process of change. Others choosing not to let go of pains of the past. From the early formative stages of life, children are taught to "stay in the lines," and do not rock the boat. We are conditioned to believe some things just are not possible. Even believers who quote the Matthew 19:26 Bible verse that says, "with God all things are possible", shrink back from taking any action when faced with the opportunities to grow that only comes through the process of change. Get Out The Way of God is a personal declaration to reaffirm that I will trust God through all the changes of life.

GET OUT THE WAY OF YOURSELF

We can all relate to making excuses about why this happened or why this did not happen. A basketball star is ejected from the game after the referee sees him punch another player. She yells out, they hit me first as if to justify and lend reasoning as to why she punched the player. The other player laughs as she walks back to her team's bench. Here is an example of the proverbial saying, "it's always the second punch that gets caught."

You might notice that excuses, in this context, are interchanged with the word reasons. Either way the attempt is made by the second player to excuse herself from any responsibility of her part in the situation. The second player feels wronged and is emotionally unable to address why she was hit in the first place. Instead of perceiving what really happened, the second player creates a story developed from an emotional interpretation which she stars in as a victim. Had the second player allowed her play on the court to speak on her behalf, she would still be playing in the game; on the court. Is your emotional state easily hurt, distracted, or manipulated? Maintain your focus on the task/purpose at hand. Get

Out the Way of your emotions and embrace the process of change so that you can be victorious in life. Choose to live in this one moment of time. Not dismissing the experiences of the past or the hope for the future, but rather understanding that living in this one moment affirms the powerful person that I Am. In this one moment, I am resilient, persistent, caring, and courageous. In fact, take a moment and appreciate yourself and everyone in your life.   Even the haters and those who treated you wrongly. Why? Because even the critics were part of the process of change that you went through and has transformed you to be strong.

GET OUT THE WAY
OF THOSE COMING AFTER YOU

You will not make progress until/unless

you are able to first accept responsibility for

the role you play in your own progress or failure. The easy thing to do is blame someone else for everything that

> "You will not make progress until/unless you are able to first accept responsibility for your part played"
> DR.MRClarke

goes wrong. This is one way of making

excuses or coming up with reasons why

something did not work. Have you ever heard

someone blame a co-worker for when things

go right? Of course, old school practitioners of

teamwork probably give people their props or

'just do.' However, today's society and culture

seem to put more emphasis on criticizing family, friends and mostly self. "It is easier to build strong children that it is to repair broken men." This quote was made by Frederick Douglass. Sadly, the opposite of Get Out the Way of those who come after is nicely exemplified in the modern-day church. There are long lines of succession waiting for the senior leader to retire or die because that's often the only way others will move up to be the head person in charge. Too often a leader will stay in the leadership position way longer than they should have. And certainly, way past any degree of effectiveness. What a sad indictment of the modern-day-church and many organizations. Rather than building up individuals and communities, the parasitic person seeks out self-serving moves that secures their own place in the organization's structure. Think about it: "I'd rather be a door keeper in the House of my God than to dwell in the tents of wickedness." Could this quote that is spoken every Sunday in many houses of Worship really mean: 'as the door keeper,' I can decide who gets in and who doesn't. I've heard of such positions in private clubs and civic organizations, but to see prejudice and racism so rampant in the church can be troubling. At the very least, self-centered, threatened leadership styles prohibit the process of change. No wonder there are fewer and fewer people going to church these days.

The relevancy of the church now rests in the cistern of society and the people perish because there is no substantive vision being offered. When organizations resist change, real growth and progress are rarely realized. Hope you will accept the concepts and conclusions of Get Out the Way. These insights can be applied to all non-profits and any organizational culture.

Get Out the Way is mostly directed at 'old guard mindsets' who fix themselves as self-authorized gate keepers of progress and growth. The old guard mindset is unable and unwilling to change. Unable to change because they are not interested in growing the mind through a deeper study of the Creator's Concepts and Principles of Life. Unwilling to change because they have no place to go. Thinking, incorrectly, that embracing change will put them out of a job. These road blockers to change never realize that by embracing the process of change, they are better equipped and positioned to lead the organization on the journey. Embracing change will empower those who come after you to succeed and do even greater deeds.

Getting out the way of progress has everything to do with understanding the state of where we are. Too many relationships and organizations rush through the process of change. Too many people settle for someone that brings no value to the relationship or an organization. Too many organizations will allow persons to remain in positions that are draining resources and undermining the success of the mission. There is a principle that captures the complex state of personal and organizational relationships regarding change. The 1969 book is called the <u>Peter Principle</u>. Developed by Laurence J. Peter, the concept is used in management that outlines how people in a hierarchy tend to rise to their "level of incompetence". <u>The Peter Principle</u> describes that "an employee is promoted based on his/her success in previous jobs until they reach a level at which he/she is no longer competent". Laurence Peter says this is because "skills in one job do not necessarily translate to another". This should sound

familiar to some if not all of you. I know it
sounds familiar to me!

How many times has a relative been
given senior leadership positions without
earning the job much less knowing how to do
the job? There are many examples in religious
organizations of ministers getting a pastoral
promotion to a large church. Let us just say,
not based on their abilities. Fraternal affiliation
is used to include frat and exclude all others.
This very same discrimination and abuse used
by America during the Reconstruction Era and
Jim Crow, that brought about the creation of
many civic organizations, is used by those who
have now become the massa and see
themselves as gods kneeling on the necks of

others. Sure, a small percentage will do ok, but the vast majority of those who's elevation was not based on merit but instead on familiarity, contributes more so to moving the organization away from its mission. A lot of people have left and are moving away from religious and civic organizations mostly due to these groups having become irrelevant. Organizations become irrelevant partly when its purpose of creation is no longer solving a problem or meeting a need. Mostly, an organization becomes irrelevant because leadership is unable to recognize the initial mission has been completed. Non-relevance occurs when the leadership becomes more focused on memorializing the accomplishments, memories, and traditions of the past. Someone once said, "tradition is frozen success." Whoever said this is right on point. Included in success is the idea that some goal or mission has been achieved. If organizational focus is only on the success and no longer 'what's next' on the agenda, then the opportunity to address the current needs of the community or market or relationships are lost. Before you take offense to my indictment of organizational non-relevance, ask yourself these questions.

Why was the organization created?

____

____

Do we celebrate anniversaries more than the

Vision forward? Give an example.

____

____

Is membership stuck in a declining trend line?

What are the current numbers?

____

____

____

During a pandemic, did anyone even know

your organization is alive and not dead?

____

Back to the point of <u>The Peter Principle</u>.
I touched on the non-relevance of

organizations experiencing decline back several paragraphs ago on page 35. Persons promoted only because of who they know, get in the way of change, progress, and growth of the organization. Sadly, if a business were to select leaders solely based on nepotism, which is the act of hiring persons related but not qualified, the business would not be in business very long. Oh, wait a minute, many non-profits and religious organizations mirror companies in the secular world in promotion by way of favor and not merit. That is, if I like you then I will give you the position out of the abundance of my greatness. Does this sound narcistic to you? Can you see how this type of narcissistic trait can disable an organization, and for that matter any relationship of not being able to embrace change? Seasons go by and no growth is apparent. All because organizations and people choose not to Get Out the Way of those generations coming after them.

Going Forward requires an honest examination of relationships and organizations focusing on whether the actions being taken are in line with the purpose and function of the stated visions and goals. In other words, the organization will operate against change and growth by having the wrong people in the wrong positions thinking that skills in one position will translate to another position. Having the wrong people in the wrong positions based on anything other than merit is all in an effort to maintain the status quo. Having the right people in the wrong position also shows an inability of leadership to understand how to implement the vision and mission of the organization towards success. When change is not seen as an important part of growth, the end result will always turn out to be one of incompetence. This is what *the Peter Principle* describes as "every position becoming occupied by someone who is incompetent in that role." Get Out the Way organizations! Get Out the Way of not allowing innovation to make a home in your company's culture. Resist the tendency to not change your packaging and hold on to outdated strategies. The times are changing

whether you like it or not.

Get Out the Way speaks to any

person(s) and organization(s) that want to see

the populace enslaved and impoverished. I

ask you again to, "Get Out the Way." Too

many people call themselves living when they

are really blind and unaware of the power of

community. Desperately holding onto the 'I

can do it on my own mindset,' many live

isolated and alone operating as consumers of

the state instead of citizens. The powers that

be, give a little crumb from the table of the

economy and we think we have arrived. Far

from it! Elite powers that be and principalities

think Black and Brown people have no skills

(vocational trade removed from high schools);
do not own property or land, and do not
produce anything of scalable worth. Without
realizing the subtle effects
of socialized dummying
down, ethnic groups
associate their acceptance
into a free and fair
democracy based on what
kind of car they drive or how many new shoes
they own. Never mind you can only drive one
car at a time or where one pair of shoes at a
time. From now on citizen, when you hear
"Get Out the Way," receive it as a clarion call
to be better; to do better.

> "The reasonable man adapts himself to the world; the unreasonable one persists in trying to adapt the world to himself..
> G.B. Shaw

So, Get Out the Way of leadership and religious folk who twist a religion and faith together to pimp people into believing more in some personality up on a stage than the Great Creator of All. Insecure status quo leaders focus is on their own job security rather than on sharing God's Truth that empowers people towards righteous living according to the Creator's precepts. Their focus is on manmade self-serving tricks that keep the people ignorant, and the organization institutionalized. To be clear, the distinction is being made between purpose driven ministry *organisms* and religious *organizations* whose

> …Therefore, all progress depends on the unreasonable man."
> G. B. Shaw

leadership has a form of godliness only. A change in direction will happen when you Get Out their Way. The question is, will each of you be prepared for inevitable change? More importantly, is leadership preparing the masses to be ready for what comes next? Too many would answer with a resounding no! To paraphrase an old saying I heard in history class. We will accept only what we are prepared to receive.

The early New Testament Church played a significant part as a body for social change. The post-civil war church in America grew and thrived because it served as an agent of change and stood up against all oppression and ideologies of the oppressing class. Unlike religious meetings today, the early church met to apply and activate strategies and principles that would feed the hungry, clothe the needy, and provide for the poor. In other words, the early church created community. "And sold their possessions and goods, and parted them to all men, as every man had need."(Acts 2.45, KJV); "Neither was there any among them that lacked: for as many as were possessors of lands or houses sold them, and brought the prices of the things that were sold."(Acts 4.34, KJV); "A feast is made for laughter, and wine maketh merry: but money answereth all things."(Eccl 10.19, KJV); also, "then she came and told the man of God. And he said, Go, sell the oil, and pay thy debt, and live thou and thy children of

the rest."(2Kings 4.7, KJV). Non-profit growth
and organizations will be more effective when
their activities include teaching people how to
fish and not only giving them fish to eat so that
each person can reproduce goodness in their
lives. In other words, scripture is full of
examples where communities were built up to
take care of the residents. Government's role
was to provide security both outside and
inside of the territory.

Get Out the Way goes out to all who do
not understand that today's non-profit and
religious organizations have a purpose which
is to facilitate the establishment of God's
Kingdom here on Earth. One criticism of
today's religious and civic organizations is that

they have lost their relevance. Another

criticism is that the church has devolved from a

thriving 'organism' into an 'organization'.

Losing one's relevance is easy to understand as

well as resolve. When an organization loses its

relevance, this simply means it has stopped

doing what the organization was organized to

do. Solving the matter of toxic leadership

intentionally devolving an institution or

organization into a stagnant existence is

somewhat more complicated to grasp as well

as restore. However, understanding the

insights of why people and organizations resist

the process of change outline in Get Out The

Way, will serve you well. Now, Live Forward,

applying coping skills that result in

transformative change.

Going Fwd is about not allowing the

dysfunction and "We cannot change
the events of the
dis-ease of past past, but we can
choose how we live
culture (accepted in the present"
DR.MRClarke
norms of behavior)   to

affect negatively, the choices of the present,

which impacts directly, the results in the

future. Every relationship and organization

must operate out of the consciousness that we

each walk in the power of the moment to effect

change in relationships and in our businesses

and organizations. "We cannot change the

events of the past, but we can choose how we

live in the present."

ABOUT THE AUTHOR

Dr.MRClarke has travelled the World to include pastoring seven congregations on three continents. He co-founded a private Christian Academy for students ages six to fifteen and several non-profit community development projects.

Dr.MRClarke served in the U.S. Navy as a Chaplain for seven years. His experience includes serving at a submarine base; a West PAC tour and two deployments to Operation Enduring Freedom and Iraqi Freedom serving with the U.S. Marines and received an Honorable Discharge.

Dr.MRClarke is a renowned innovator and trailblazer who, to date, has one Bachelor,

two Masters, and two Doctorate degrees. Dr.
Clarke earned a B.A. degree in Accounting
from Morehouse College in Atlanta, Georgia; a
Masters of Divinity from the
Interdenominational Theological Center in
Atlanta, Georgia; a Masters of Arts degree in
National Security and Strategic Studies from
the United States of America Naval War
College in Newport, Rhode Island; an
Associates of Science degree from Florida State
College Jacksonville in Supply Chain
Management; a Doctor of Divinity degree from
Andersonville Seminary in Georgia and a 2nd
Doctor of Divinity degree from the
Interdenominational Theological Center where
the DMin Project was entitled:

<u>Ministry Economic Empowerment: A Non-Traditional Fundraising Project Towards Ministry Growth</u>.

Dr.MRClarke previously held a mortgage broker license and currently is a Licensed Independent Life, Health and Mutual Insurance Agent and founder of the ARC Agency. A non-profit whose mission is to educate communities and advocate for Life & Health Insurance be included in all family legacy plans. Do NOT leave Final Expense Debt upon your death. Contact DR.MRClarke for your personal consultation via social media or at XinJinse@gmail.com.

Thank You

for taking the time to read

Get Out the Way.

Blessings to You!

DR. MRCLARKE

Made in the USA
Monee, IL
07 July 2026

56552163R00066